# Swimmers

Powell, Jillian.
    Swimmers / by Jillian Powell.
        p.  cm.
    First published 1991 by Firefly Books, Ltd., Hove, East Sussex.
    Summary: Depicts animals that spend some or all of their time
in the water and describes how they swim.
    ISBN 0-87614-703-1
    1. Animal swimming—Juvenile literature. [1. Animal swimming.
2. Aquatic animals.] I. Title.
QP310.S95P68   1991
591.1'852—dc20                                          91-18842
                                                           CIP
                                                            AC

Printed in Belgium by Casterman S.A.
Bound in the United States of America

1  2  3  4  5  6  7  8  9  10  01  00  99  98  97  96  95  94  93  92

## THINGS THAT MOVE

# Swimmers

Written by Jillian Powell

Carolrhoda Books, Inc./Minneapolis

Ducklings start to swim soon after hatching. They follow the mother duck, pushing themselves through the water with their webbed feet.

Baby frogs swim like fish.  But as adults, frogs swim by kicking with their long back legs as if they were hopping on land.

Fish are among the fastest
swimmers in the world.  They
bend their tails from side to side,
wriggling through the water.

Dogs swim using their front and back legs to paddle. People "dog-paddle" when they swim with their heads above water.

Many animals are able to swim when they are born, but people must learn how to swim. These children are having fun at their swimming lesson!

Divers can swim underwater, using flippers
to push themselves along.  They wear special
diving suits that keep them warm, and they
breathe using scuba gear.

Some beetles live in the water. The great diving beetle lives in ponds. Its back legs are covered with tiny hairs that help push it through the water.

Penguins can't fly. Instead, they use their wings like flippers to dive and swim.

Many snakes are good swimmers. A snake swims by wriggling and bending its body like a fish does.

Newts live in ponds, lakes, and streams. They swim by moving their bodies and tails.

Sea lions have smooth bodies
and flippers that help them
swim quickly.  Their back
flippers are used to steer.

Dolphins live in the ocean. They jump and swim in the water, playing and feeding on fish.

Marine turtles live mainly in the ocean and swim using their front flippers. They come on land only to sleep or to lay their eggs in the sand.

Crocodiles can crawl on land or swim in the water. Their eyes are high on their heads so that they can see their prey while staying hidden in the water.

Polar bears can swim a long way in order to find food. They have thick coats and layers of fat to keep them warm in the icy water.

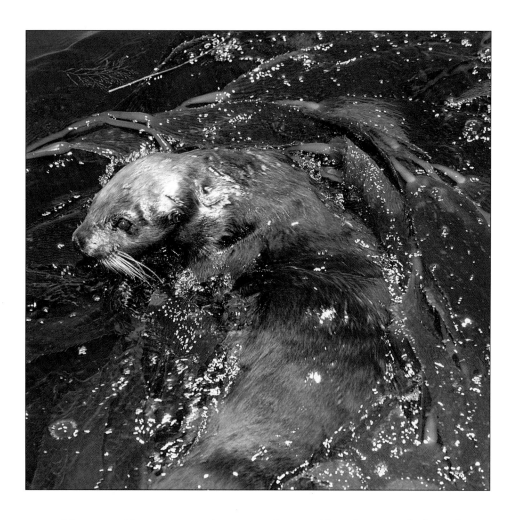

Sea otters swim using their webbed
back feet and thick tails.  They dive
to catch fish and shellfish.

Beavers live in rivers and streams
near wooded areas.  They build dams
underwater out of tree branches.

Some people learn to swim and dive underwater. They must come to the surface when they need to breathe.

A jellyfish swims by opening its body
like an umbrella and then closing it
quickly to push itself through the water.
Some jellyfish can give painful stings.

An octopus swims backward by squirting water from a hole under its head. It uses its eight tentacles to crawl over rocks.

# Read about other
# *THINGS THAT MOVE:*

# *Climbers*

# *Flyers*

# *Jumpers*

**Photo acknowledgments**

The photographs in this book were supplied by: pp. 4 (S. Neilson), 7 (Jane Burton), 14 (Frans Lanting), 15 (main photo, Hans Reinhard), 16 (Jane Burton), 19 (Jeff Foot), 22 (M.P. Price), 23 (Jane Burton), Bruce Coleman Ltd.; p. 11 (main pic., A. Bannister), NHPA; pp. 5 (Terry Heathcote), 6 (Colin Milkins), 10 (Colin Milkins), 11 (inset, Raymond Blyth), 12 (Raymond Blyth), 13 (G.I. Bernard), 17 (G.I. Bernard), 18 (Margot Conte), 20 (Michael Leach), Oxford Scientific Films; pp. 9, 15 (inset), 21, ZEFA.

24